CHEETAHS

Ann Baggaley

Grolier
an imprint of

www.scholastic.com/librarypublishing

Published 2009 by Grolier
An imprint of Scholastic Library Publishing
Old Sherman Turnpike, Danbury,
Connecticut 06816

For The Brown Reference Group plc
Project Editor: Jolyon Goddard
Picture Researcher: Clare Newman
Designers: Dave Allen, Jeni Child, Lynne Ross,
    Sarah Williams
Managing Editors: Bridget Giles, Tim Harris

Volume ISBN-13: 978-0-7172-6289-2
Volume ISBN-10: 0-7172-6289-8

**Library of Congress
Cataloging-in-Publication Data**

Nature's children. Set 4.
    p. cm.
  Includes bibliographical references and
  index.
  ISBN 13: 978-0-7172-8083-4
  ISBN 10: 0-7172-8083-7 ((set 4) : alk. paper)
  1. Animals--Encyclopedias, Juvenile. I.
  Grolier (Firm)
  QL49.N385 2009
  590.3--dc22
                        2007046315

Printed and bound in China

Contents

Fact File: Cheetahs 4

Close Relatives 7

Not Such a Big Cat 8

A Lot of Spots 11

Roaming the Plains 12

Cheetah History 15

Record Breakers 16

Keeping Still 19

The Cat That Barks 20

Favorite Food 23

Daytime Hunters 24

Prowling Thieves 25

Feature Photo 26–27

Teeth and Whiskers 28

Claws and Paws 31

Single Girls 32

Sociable Males 35

Nap Time 36

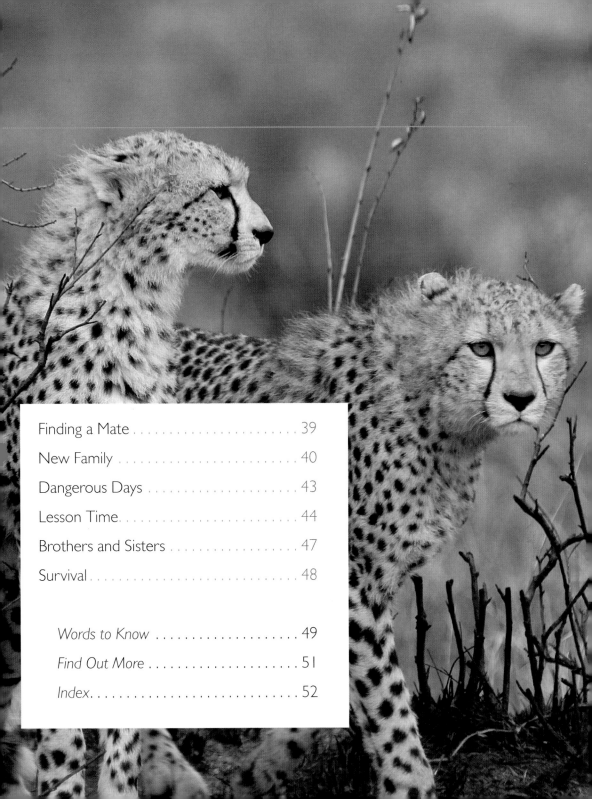

Finding a Mate 39

New Family 40

Dangerous Days 43

Lesson Time. 44

Brothers and Sisters 47

Survival 48

Words to Know 49

Find Out More 51

Index. 52

FACT FILE: Cheetahs

Class	Mammals (Mammalia)
Order	Carnivores (Carnivora)
Family	Cats (Felidae)
Genus	*Acinonyx*
Species	Cheetahs (*Acinonyx jubatus*)
World distribution	Africa and Iran
Habitat	Grasslands, dry forests, and semideserts
Distinctive physical characteristics	Tan coat with small black spots; "tear stripe" markings on face; long legs; blunt, nonretractable claws
Habits	Hunt by day; stalk prey then chase at high speed; females live and raise cubs alone; males form small groups
Diet	Small antelope, warthogs, hares, rabbits, and birds

Introduction

The cheetah has been called "the fastest animal on four legs." It is certainly built to be the world's champion sprinter—its legs are amazingly long for a cat and also extremely powerful. Cheetahs not only look different from all their cat relatives, they behave differently, too. Cheetahs hunt by day, instead of prowling in search of **prey** by night. They can't climb trees very well because they don't have sharp claws. And they make noises that sound like a dog or even a bird!

Cheetahs have about 2,000 spots on their coat.

The caracal, which lives in Africa and Asia, is a small cat with highly distinctive ear tufts.

Close Relatives

The cheetah belongs to the cat family. There are 37 different **species**, or types, of cat, both big and small. Cheetahs are regarded as big cats, like lions, tigers, leopards, and jaguars. Small cats include domestic cats and many different wild species from all over the world. Among the best known of these small cats are the beautifully patterned ocelot from South America and the thick-furred lynx, which are found in the northern forests of America, Europe, and Asia. Lynx also live in Spain and Portugal.

Scientists think that cheetahs first **evolved** into a separate species of the cat family about four million years ago. They also think that the cheetahs living today might all be descended from a very small number of original **ancestors** that survived the last Ice Age, about 10,000 years ago. In scientific tests, all cheetahs are shown to be very closely related to one another.

Not Such a Big Cat

Although the cheetah is called a "big" cat, it is actually much smaller than other big cats such as the lion and the tiger. And its streamlined body, as long-legged and slender as that of a greyhound dog, makes it look very different from a leopard—even though they both have a spotted coat.

An adult cheetah weighs between 86 and 143 pounds (40 to 65 kg), and measures 3½ to 4½ feet (1 to 1.4 m) from head to rear. The long tail adds another 2 to 3½ feet (0.6 to 1 m) to the animal's total length. A cheetah stands about 2 to 3 feet (0.6 to 0.9 m) tall, measured from the ground to the top of its shoulder.

Male cheetahs are usually slightly bigger than the females. However, both males and females vary in size, so it is not always easy to tell them apart.

A mother cheetah and her cubs get a good view of their surroundings from the top of a termite mound.

9

King cheetahs are rare in the wild—the first time one was photographed was in 1974.

A Lot of Spots

A cheetah's fur is golden tan on its upper parts, and marked with small, round black spots. Each cheetah has a different pattern of spots. The animal's underparts are pale gray or white. Its tail has black rings toward the end and at the tip there is a tuft of white hair. The cheetah's coat is short. The coat might look silky, but it actually feels rough to the touch.

The cheetah has a small head with little rounded ears. Its face is marked with distinctive black lines, like tear streaks, that run down both sides of the nose from the inner corners of the eyes. It is thought that these marks help keep the glare of the sun out of the cheetah's eyes.

A few, very rare cheetahs have a coat patterned with large black blotches instead of spots. Those animals are called king cheetahs. Despite their unusual markings, king cheetahs are not a different species.

Roaming the Plains

Most cheetahs live in the **plains** of Africa.
Cheetah country includes the vast Serengeti
of Tanzania and the grasslands of Namibia. In
those regions, cheetahs have plenty of space to
roam, and there is an abundance of the animals
that cheetahs hunt for food. The tall grass that
covers the plains is ideal for cheetahs to hide in
when they are stalking prey. Cheetahs also live
in open woodland and semidesert areas. They
like places where there are rocks they can climb
to look out over their surroundings.

Though very rare, a few cheetahs are found
in northern Iran. It is thought that no more
than 100 of them still exist in isolated pockets
of the country.

Like most predators, cheetahs have forward-facing eyes that allow the cat to judge distances accurately when chasing down prey.

This copy of an ancient Egyptian painting shows a cheetah accompanying a hunting party.

Cheetah History

Thousands of years ago, cheetahs were much more widespread than they are today. Cheetahs once existed all over North America, Europe, India, and in many other parts of Asia, as well as Africa.

The cheetah got its name in India, where it was found until the 1950s—now the cheetah is **extinct** in that country. In the Hindi language, the word *chita*, which eventually became "cheetah," means "spotted one." Wealthy Indian rulers once kept tame cheetahs and trained them to hunt for sport.

In fact, the cheetah has a long history of being held in captivity. The ancient Egyptian pharaohs used to keep them as pets and symbols of royalty. In India as well as other countries, cheetahs were tamed as hunting animals. From the 5th century onward, for hundreds of years, princes and noblemen from many countries, including Italy, Russia, France, and China, used these animals to hunt other animals.

Record Breakers

The cheetah can run faster than any other animal in the world. It can go from a standstill to 45 miles (72 km) per hour in just three seconds, and has a top speed of about 60 miles (95 km) per hour. But a cheetah can only keep up its top speed for about 30 seconds. It then has to stop because its body gets too hot and it runs out of breath!

Every part of the cheetah's body is ideal for running fast. Long legs and an extra long backbone let this cat stretch out and cover 7 to 8 feet (2 to 2.5 m) with each stride. The cheetah's tail acts as a balancing pole to stop it from falling over when it makes sharp turns at high speeds.

To help it even more, the cheetah has large lungs and a large heart that supply its body with plenty of oxygen for fuel. Even the cheetah's nose is useful for an animal that runs so fast, because it has wide nostrils that take in air very quickly.

Cheetahs can run faster than all their prey.

Cheetahs mainly use vision for hunting, but they can also detect prey by smell.

Keeping Still

Running fast is not the only thing that cheetahs are very good at. They are also skilled at keeping absolutely still. When a cheetah senses danger, it "freezes" and can stay almost entirely motionless for nearly half an hour.

The art of freezing helps the cheetah when it is out hunting. It is hard for any **predator** to stalk an animal without letting it know that an enemy is approaching. By staying completely still, the cheetah has a good chance that its prey will come close without noticing any danger. When a cheetah freezes, its spotted fur helps keep the cat concealed. If the cheetah doesn't move, the pattern of the coat is very hard to see in the long grass. Of course, if the prey catches scent of the cheetah, then the trick doesn't work!

The Cat That Barks

Some of the noises a cheetah makes are just like those of a pet cat. The cheetah purrs when it is contented and hisses and spits when it is angry or frightened. Female cheetahs and their young also make birdlike chirruping sounds to each other.

Unlike the other big cats, a cheetah cannot roar. To communicate with others of its kind, the cheetah makes a sound that is most unusual for a cat—it barks.

Cheetahs call with a high-pitched, far-carrying yelp or yap. If cheetahs meet, they "talk" to each other using various barking noises. Different barking sounds mean different things. For instance, a male cheetah will make one type of bark to give a friendly welcome to a female. Cheetahs also have a warning bark to tell strangers not to enter their territory. A third kind of bark says they don't want to fight.

A barking cheetah
shows off its tongue.
Like all cats, the tongue
is rough and can rasp
meat off bones.

In the Serengeti, gazelles make up 90 percent of the cheetah's prey.

Favorite Food

Cheetahs are **carnivores**—animals that eat only meat. Their favorite prey includes small antelope, such as gazelles and impalas, and the young of larger hoofed animals, such as wildebeest. They also catch the young of warthogs—a type of wild pig commonly found in the African plains—as well as hares, rabbits, and sometimes birds.

An adult cheetah eats about 4½ pounds (2 kg) of meat a day, when the hunting is good. But these cats don't need to drink very much. Cheetahs can easily go for three or four days without water. During the times of year when there is little or no rain, and many water holes dry up completely, cheetahs can survive without drinking anything for more than a week.

Daytime Hunters

Cheetahs go hunting during the daytime, usually either in the early morning or late in the afternoon, when it is not too hot. Adult cheetahs always hunt alone.

To search the plains for prey, a cheetah stands on a high spot, such as a rock. When it sees a possible victim—perhaps a warthog or a gazelle that has strayed from its herd—it begins to stalk. Crouching low and moving stealthily through the grass, the cheetah creeps up on its prey. When it is about 30 yards (27 m) away, the cheetah springs from hiding and chases its prey at top speed. Because the cheetah can only run at top speed for about half a minute, the intended victim often escapes. At least half of all hunts end in failure for the cheetah. But if the cheetah is successful, it pulls the prey down and seizes it by the throat.

Prowling Thieves

There are more dangerous predators than the cheetah living on the plains, including lions, leopards, and hyenas. But they rarely attack an adult cheetah. They do, however, often make life hard for the cheetah by stealing its food. They watch as a cheetah catches its prey and then move in to grab a free meal. Faced with rivals that are much stronger than itself, the cheetah is forced to back away and go hungry.

A cheetah with a fresh kill must also keep a lookout for vultures that might be circling overhead. Those huge birds do not catch their own prey, so they are always waiting for the opportunity to snatch someone else's meal. A cheetah often drags its kill to a sheltered place, such as under a bush, so that it has a chance to eat in peace.

The cheetah is not the smallest of the big cats—it is bigger than the snow leopard and the two species of clouded leopards.

Teeth and Whiskers

For a big cat, a cheetah has relatively small teeth. Because of that, when it catches large prey, such as an antelope, it cannot bite as far through its prey's skin as a lion or a tiger can to make a kill. Instead, the cheetah holds on to the throat of its victim in a tight grip until the animal suffocates.

The cheetah also has small whiskers compared to the very long whiskers usually seen on other members of the cat family. Cats use those long whiskers like feelers to sense what is around them, especially when they are hunting in the dark—which is what most cats do. The cheetah is usually out and about during the daytime, so it can easily see where it is going and doesn't need whiskers to help guide itself.

Like all cats, a cheetah's sharp teeth are suited to biting, stabbing, and cutting.

Claws are made of a tough substance called keratin. Keratin is also the main ingredient of hair, fingernails, hooves, horns, and feathers.

30

Claws and Paws

Most cats, both big and small, have **retractable** claws. That means the claws can be pulled back into pockets of skin and fur, called **sheaths**, in their paws. The cheetah is unusual because it cannot draw its claws all the way in. A cheetah's claws can always been seen, like those of a dog.

A cheetah has a hooked claw, called a **dewclaw**, on the inside of each front leg. The dewclaw helps the cheetah to catch hold of its prey. All its other claws are only slightly curved, and they are blunt—again more like a dog's than a cat's claws, which are usually curved and sharp. The blunt claws grip the ground well, so they help the cheetah stay on its feet as it runs, twisting and turning after prey. To give extra grip, the pads on a cheetah's paws have small ridges.

Single Girls

Female cheetahs always live alone, except when they are bringing up their young. They don't mark out a particular territory, but they do have home ranges. Those ranges often cover enormous areas, sometimes as much as 300 square miles (800 sq km). Throughout the year, females roam their home range, following herds of prey animals, such as gazelles, as they travel in search of new grass.

Female cheetahs' home ranges are far too big for them to defend against intruders. So one female's range usually overlaps that of another female's, often a close relative, such as a mother, daughter, or sister. Neighboring female cheetahs rarely meet. The only time adult females spend time with other adult cheetahs is when they are ready to **mate**.

Female cheetahs live to about 12 years in the wild. Males usually reach about 9 years. In zoos, cheetahs can live to 15 years.

The males in a coalition get along well, although they might squabble over kills and which one gets to mate with female cheetahs.

Sociable Males

Unlike the females, most male cheetahs like company, though some do live alone. It is common for two or three males, which are usually related to one another, to form a group. The group of males, which is called a coalition (CO-AH-LISH-UN), stays together for life.

The males in a coalition often mark out a small territory of about 15 square miles (37 sq km) by spraying their urine on trees or other landmarks such as rocks. They fiercely defend their territory, attacking any lone male that happens to cross the boundary. Such fights between males sometimes end in one of the cheetahs being seriously injured or even killed. A group of males might hold a territory for four years or more. However, they are always at risk of being driven out by a stronger coalition.

Nap Time

What does a cheetah do when it is not out hunting? During the middle of the day, when the sun is hot in the African plains, cheetahs spend many hours sleeping or just resting in the shade of a tree.

Like all cats, cheetahs are fussy about keeping themselves clean. They often use their leisure time to groom themselves. Male cheetahs that live in groups often help one another with this task. They lick each other around the head and behind the ears. Friendly grooming like that is not just about cleanliness. It also helps the group bond.

Cheetahs prefer not to get their fur wet, but they do enjoy a dust bath. Rolling around in the dust removes many of the fleas and other pests that get into the cheetah's coat and cause itching.

Cheetahs sleep at night and also take several naps during the day.

A male and female cheetah are very affectionate toward each other for the short time they spend together.

Finding a Mate

Cheetahs are ready to find a mate when they are about 18 months to two years old. However, the males are not likely to be successful at courting for another year or two after that. These cats do not have a particular mating season and breed at any time of year.

To attract males, the female cheetah leaves scent marks throughout her range by spraying urine on trees and other landmarks. When a male picks up her scent, he follows the trail to find her and mate with her. After mating, the pair do not stay together for long, though they might spend a day or two grooming each other or playing. The female then returns to her solitary way of life and the male, unless he is solitary too, goes back to his group.

New Family

About three months after mating, the female cheetah looks for a safe place to give birth to her young, or **cubs**. She usually chooses a **lair** in thick, tall grass or among rocks.

The cubs are born tiny, blind, and helpless. There are normally three or four cubs in a **litter**. But some mothers have only one cub while others have as many as eight.

The cubs' eyes first open when they are about ten days old. At first, they have a fluffy gray, spotted coat and a long mane of gray hair, called a **mantle**, that grows over their neck, shoulders, and back. Some scientists think that the mantle might help hide the cubs in the grass. Other people have suggested that the long hair deters predators by making the cubs look like bigger, fiercer animals. When the cubs get older the mantle gradually disappears and their gray fur lightens to tan.

A five-day-old cub knows to keep quiet and still as its mother moves it to another lair.

41

At three weeks old, a cheetah cub's teeth break through its gums.

Dangerous Days

During their early days, young cubs **nurse** on their mother's milk and are kept well hidden in the lair. That is a dangerous time for the cubs because they are at great risk of being attacked by predators, especially lions. To make it harder for such predators to hunt young cheetah cubs, the mother moves her litter to a different lair every few days.

Male cheetahs do not help guard the cubs. The mother has to leave them unprotected while she goes hunting to find food for herself. That is when predators are most likely to turn up. In areas where there are large numbers of lions, such as the Serengeti, most cheetah cubs do not survive their first year of life.

When the cubs are six to eight weeks old, they are strong enough to follow their mother beyond the lair. At this time they start to eat small amounts of meat, though they continue to nurse from their mother for several more weeks.

Lesson Time

At three or four months old, cheetah cubs stop drinking their mother's milk and feed only on meat. The mother cheetah now takes her cubs with her when she goes hunting. She shows them what to do and how to recognize which animals are good prey.

As the young cheetahs grow bigger and stronger, they join in the hunt. Sometimes, though, the excited youngsters just get in the way. Their mother then has no chance of catching anything.

Cheetah cubs also develop their hunting skills by play-fighting with one another. They even practice catching prey by mock-attacking their mother and seizing her neck with their teeth. Those games are fun, but they are very important lessons for the young animals, too. They need to learn as much as they can before it's time for them to live on their own.

A mother cheetah inspects her cub's hunting skills as it chases a baby gazelle.

Two young cheetahs
explore the burnt ground
after a savanna fire.

Brothers and Sisters

When young cheetahs are around 18 months old, their mother leaves them. But the litter stays together as a group for a few months longer. The young adult cheetahs are often still not very skilled at hunting or looking after themselves. They often make mistakes, such as chasing animals that are far too big for them to kill. Living with brothers and sisters gives them all a better chance of survival.

Eventually, the females break away from the group one by one to find a range and roam the plains alone. Each female then stays by herself until she mates and has cubs of her own. The brothers are more likely to have formed close bonds and so they will probably remain together. That is how most male coalitions are formed.

Survival

If a cheetah survives the first year of its life, it might live for up to 12 years. But even an adult cheetah does not find life easy.

The cheetah has to compete for prey against larger predators, such as the lion, but this is not its only challenge. Humans are the biggest threat to the cheetah. For centuries, men hunted the cheetah for its fur. Because of that, the total number of cheetahs alive today is very small. Scientists think that there are no more than about 15,000 cheetahs left in the wild. It is now against the law in most countries to sell cheetah skins, but **poachers** still catch the cubs to sell as pets. Another problem is that much of the cheetahs' homeland has been turned into farmland. Cheetahs are often illegally shot or trapped by farmers who fear they will attack their cattle.

However, many organizations are working to protect the cheetah. With their help, this beautiful cat will hopefully survive for a long time to come.

Words to Know

Ancestors   Early types of an existing species.

Carnivores   Mammals that eat only, or mainly, meat.

Cubs   Young cheetahs.

Dewclaw   A claw, separate from the other claws, on the back of an animal's lower front leg.

Evolved   Developed gradually over many generations and thousands of years.

Extinct   When all of a species are dead and gone forever.

Lair   A sheltered place where an animal rests or raises its young.

Litter   Young animals born to the same mother at the same time.

Mantle	The long fur on a young cheetah's neck, shoulders, and back.
Mate	To come together to produce young.
Nurse	To feed on a mother's milk.
Plains	Level, open country with few trees.
Poachers	People who hunt illegally.
Predator	An animal that hunts other animals.
Prey	An animal hunted by another animal for food.
Retractable	Describing claws that an animal can draw back into its paws.
Sheaths	Pockets of skin in an animal's paws into which it can pull its claws.
Species	The scientific word for animals of the same type that can breed together.

Find Out More

Books

Squire, A. O. *Cheetahs*. True Books. Animals. Danbury, Connecticut: Children's Press, 2005.

Theodorou, R. *Cheetah*. Animals in Danger. Chicago, Illinois: Heinemann Library, 2002.

Web sites

Cheetah Conservation Fund: Coloring Book
www.cheetah.org/?nd=kids-01
A lot of pictures of cheetahs to print and color in.

Creature Feature: Cheetahs
www.nationalgeographic.com/kids/creature_feature/0003/cheetah2.html
Fun facts, an audio clip, a video, and links to other cheetah web sites.

Index

A, B, C

Africa 6, 12, 15, 23, 36

Asia 6, 7, 15

barking 20, 21

big cats 7, 8, 27, 28

birth 40

caracal 6

cat family 7

claws 5, 30, 31

climbing 5

coalition 34, 35, 47

coat 5, 8, 11, 36, 40

communication 20

courting 38, 39

cubs 9, 40, 41, 42, 43, 44, 45, 47, 48

D, E, F

dewclaw 31

drinking 23

dust bath 36

ears 11, 36

evolution 7

eyes 11, 13, 40

eyesight 18

fighting 20, 35

fur 11, 19, 31, 36, 48

G, H

gazelles 22, 23, 32, 45

grooming 36, 39

habitat 12

head 11, 16, 36

height 8

home range 32

hunting 5, 12, 14, 15, 18, 23, 24, 28, 44, 45, 47

K, L, M

keratin 30

king cheetah 10, 11

lair 40, 41, 43

legs 5, 8, 16

length 8

life span 33, 48

litter 40, 43, 47

mantle 40

mating 32, 34, 39, 40, 47

milk 43, 44

N, P, R

nose 16

nursing 43

paws 31

play 39, 44

poaching 48

predators 13, 19, 24, 40, 43, 48

prey 5, 12, 13, 19, 22, 23, 24, 25, 28, 31, 32, 44

roaring 20

running 5, 16, 19, 24, 31

S, T, U

skin 31

sleep 36, 37

small cats 7

smell 18

speed 16, 17, 24

stalking 24

tail 8, 11, 16

teeth 28, 29, 42, 44

territory 20, 35

tongue 21

urine 35, 39

W, Z

weight 8

whiskers 28

zoos 33